HOW TO TURN YOUR TEACHER PURPLE!

SiZZLiNG SCieNCe PoeMs

CHOSEN BY
JaMes CaRteR

Illus

D1136187

*For the family that fizzes with elemental energy,
the 4Browns4: Ian, Annie, Ella and Daniel.*

With many thanks to Paul Finburg of CCFE in Culham,
Michael Huffer of SLAC National Laboratory USA,
Graham Denton, Nick Arnold, Kate Paice, Rachel Kellehar,
Ruth Dix, bat enthusiast Pete Kaspar, the Royal Observatory
and the Science Museum.
In memory of my inspirational Biology teacher, Mr Tim Potts.

First published 2011 by
A & C Black Publishers Ltd
36 Soho Square, London, W1D 3QY

www.acblack.com

Collection copyright © 2011 James Carter
Illustrations copyright © 2011 Nigel Baines

The rights of James Carter and Nigel Baines to be identified
as the editor and illustrator of this work have been asserted by them
in accordance with the Copyrights, Designs and Patents Act 1988.

ISBN 978-1-4081-2648-6

A CIP catalogue for this book is available from the British Library.

This book is produced using paper that is made from wood
grown in managed, sustainable forests. It is natural, renewable
and recyclable. The logging and manufacturing processes conform
to the environmental regulations of the country of origin.

Printed and bound in Great Britain
by CPI Cox and Wyman, Reading, RG1 8EX.

CONTENTS

SHOCKING EXPERIMENTS

THE SAD, MAD PROFESSOR

COMPLETELY COSMIC!

Time is Eating the Cliffs

How Come Bees Can Fly?

WRappeD iN SkiN

A Sci-Fi DReaM

SHOCKING EXPERIMENTS

Science Stinks

Science stinks.

And that's not all.

It fizzes, flashes, bubbles, bangs,
grows, glows, pulls, pushes,
moves, murmurs, hums, growls,
crawls, creeps, bleeds, breeds,

Tries, tests, bends, breaks
makes, mends, clones, cures,
probes, peers, seeks, finds,
clears, steers, leads, links.

Don't you love it?

Science stinks!

Paul Bright

CHEMISTRY LESSON

Mix oxygen and hydrogen,
as much as you can get.
Strike a match and step right back,
or else you'll end up wet.
Mix oxygen and hydrogen,
be careful how you go;
for if you mix too much of it,
you'll drown in H_2O!

Paul Hughes

SHOCKING EXPERIMENT

A curious toddler called Doug
His thumb in a socket did plug,
And became by this science
An electric appliance
For burning a hole in the rug.

Philip Waddell

THe BUTTeRCUP EXPeRiMeNT

From the overgrown lawn I picked a buttercup
and held it under my sister's chin.
"This is the buttercup experiment," I said,
"let's see if it shines yellow on your skin."

It did. "It means you like butter."
We gathered more buttercups. The day was
   hot.
On the kitchen windowsill we arranged them
in a plastic beaker and a yoghurt pot.

How they glowed ... like little suns,
or butter on toast, or flame of candlelight!
So much brighter than the dullness of mustard
or the moon's pale face on a dark winter's
   night.

Wes Magee

HOW TO TURN YOUR TEACHER PURPLE!

Heebie geebie, hurple burple
time to turn my teacher purple!

Simply chant this magic spell.
Soon your teacher looks unwell.
Purple cheeks and purple nose.
Purpleness from head to toes.

Feed her beetroot every hour.
See her fill with purple power.
Bloomin' like a purple flower.
How she'll **SCREEEEEEEAM**
                    when in the shower!

James Carter

Green School

The school has gone green
an allotment's being made
and we're wearing wellies
and carrying spades.
We're digging the ground up,
we're planting the seeds,
we're making a compost heap
out of the weeds.
We'll be growing tomatoes
and three kinds of bean,
potatoes and pumpkins,
the biggest you've seen.
And cabbages, carrots,
cucumbers and peas,
and a few marigolds
for attracting the bees.
We're the new eco army,
all of us keen
on changing the world
now the school has gone green.

Marian Swinger

TAKE A TRIP TO THE...

Seriously
Cool
Inventions &
Exhibits:
Neutrons, nerves & nuclear stuff!
Climate, chemistry & cures!
Energy, elements & electronics!

Medicine & molecules & microscopes!
Universes, ultrasounds & UFOs!
Sound, spectrums & space!
Evolution, eclipses & environments!
Utterly & undeniably & unbelievably
Mind blowing!!!!!!!!!!

James Carter

THe SAD, MAD PROFeSSOR

CURiOSiTY KiLLeD
THe CAT

Curiosity killed the cat, they say.
I say, this proves that the cat was no scientist,
who are by their very nature, curious beings
that's what makes them scientists –
their never-ending curiosity
to find answers.
How does fire burn?
What makes a colour?
Why do we cry tears?
How far is it possible to travel?
Could we run cars on water?
Is it possible to turn straw into comfortable
    clothes?
How did they build the pyramids?
If I dug a big hole here, what would I find?
How do fish communicate?
Could we send a beam of light out into space
    that stretched forever?
What will we do when there's nowhere left
    for the rubbish?
Will we ever run out of questions?
Not as long as we have scientists
and curiosity
and cats.

Amanda Lowe

Einstein

Long years ago, nobody cared
That E was really mc^2.
Then Albert Einstein thought a bit,
And felt that he should mention it.

Colin West

ROLL ON: THE INVENTION OF THE WHEEL

"It's a massive stone," said Urg.
"It'll certainly take some shifting."
Groans from the band of labourers
At the thought of the heavy lifting.
"Just get it on the sledge," said Lurg.
"Then there's five miles of dragging."
Cue further groans from the workforce,
Spirits visibly sagging.
With stone on sledge, drag ropes tight
But hearts not really in it,
The draggers slack off thankfully
When a voice says, "Just a minute."
A girl who has been watching
Adds, "Look, you'll think I'm daft
But the shifting might be easier
On a kind of rolling raft."
She pointed to a tidy pile
Of young trees cut for burning,
All trimmed and similar in size:
"Perfect for rolling, turning."
The draggers, quick to understand,
Build up the trial raft.
The stone is mounted – push – it rolls!
Idea perhaps not so daft.

Still much work to do, of course:
As the back rollers run load-free
They're fed in at the front –
This done continuously.
"Still slow," thinks the girl with ideas
Watching the heavy movement.
"Might it be possible to make
Another big improvement...
I wonder now," she muses.
"Need the rollers be so long...
Suppose we cut round slices off...
Surely that can't be wrong?
Those round slices at the corners
Of a platform strong and flat,
With the slices free to spin and turn –
How could we manage that?
We'd need a group to work it out...
Tests... many a trial run...
But," said the girl with bright ideas,
"I think it can be done."

Eric Finney

WHAT'S WATT!

"He was Scottish!"

"Lucky him."

"And he invented steam."

"I thought the kettle did that!"

"No, I mean he helped develop the idea of
using steam in an engine."

"Well done, mastermind... So his name was?"

"It will come to me in a minute."

"I won't hold my breath as I might get
steamed up about it!"

"You can joke but he also invented the... er,
letter-copying press and..."

"What?"

"That's it!"

"What's it?"

"No, not what but Watt! A unit of electricity."

"What?"

"You just don't know what's watt around
here."

"And you don't even know what his name is!"

"Oh yes I do!"

"Go on then, tell me."

"Quite simple really!"

"Oh yes?'

"It's old Watt's-his-name!"

Ian Souter

20

EDiSON

Thomas Alva Edison invented all day long,
A fact you should remember every time you
hear a song –
For iPods and CDs, my dear, did not appear
by magic:
If Tom had not recorded sound, the loss
would have been tragic.
Though 'Mary had a little lamb' made
everybody laugh,
He revolutionised our lives with the
phonograph.
Admittedly, some others got involved along
the way
To make recordings super-special, as they are
today,
But Tom it was who thought it up. He also
rose to fame
For bringing us electric light. It wouldn't be
the same
Without his scientific skill. Thank God it was
his calling.
There's one more thing that you should know:
his spelling was appalling.

Rosemary Hodi

THe SaD, MaD PROFessOR

I'm worried, Professor, you seem very ill.
Each day you appear to be thinner.
You lie there quite silently, perfectly still,
refusing your breakfast and dinner.
I know that your submarine sun-roof went
   wrong
and drowned quite a number of men.
The balsa-wood barbecue didn't last long,
but get up and try, try again.
Your toilet-seat microphone works very well;
poor mother felt sick when I tried it.
The clockwork umbrella will certainly sell,
though grandma is still trapped inside it.
So, don't be unhappy, no, don't be
   depressed,
your genius couldn't be clearer.
I love your inventions, I'm truly impressed.
Your failures bring triumph nearer.

Paul Hughes

ELecTRic KeNNiNG

Lightning maker
electron shaker

street lamp lighter
darkness fighter

fire heater
cold defeater

crumpet toaster
Sunday roaster

blanket warmer
bed transformer

kettle boiler
constant toiler

fridge and freezer
here to please ya

Each and every home appliance
needs the wonder of my science!

Ian Brown

TiMe Piece

I spent
24 hours
trying
to
work out
what the
equivalent
of
86 thousand
and
400
seconds is,
till I
finally
decided
to
give up
and
call it
a day.

Graham Denton

COMPLETELY COSMIC!

WeLL?

Did it all begin
with a
MIGHTY DIN
and a
  CRASH
and a
    CLANG
and a
  BIG
      BIG
          BANG?

Well... some say
                no
and some say
                yes
and some say
        we can only guess...

James Carter

CReATiON

God, smiling and chuckling
at His own designs.

Knee-deep in feathers and scales
bits of beak and bone.

Elbows splattered with mud and sand,
clay and water, hair and fur.

Not so much the initial designs that impress,
original though they are.

It's what He did with the leftovers
that's real creative genius.

How else would you get an armadillo
or a duck-billed platypus?

Paul Cookson

LEFTOVER BITS

cosMic

All stuff is built of atoms.
star stuff, sand stuff, skin stuff
water vapour that you breathe out
when you sigh, tears you cry,
chips you fry, lips and lungs,
tongues, toadstools, trees,
ostriches, the rocky Pyrenees
and cheese on toast,
the sky, the sea the coast…

All stuff is made of atoms
and every atom (smaller smaller smaller
than a freckle on a freckle on a flea)
is like a mini solar system
looks just like planets
orbiting the sun.

Everything's begun in atoms,
so inside every sort of thing
is outer space in miniature.
How cool, how weird is that?
A speck contains a million
spinning suns…
and inside everything
is space.

Jan Dean

THiNk OF iT

Think of the hugeness of the universe.
Think of the enormous number of stars.
Think of the planets revolving round
    those stars.

But most of them are
    too close to their sun (too hot!)
    too far from their sun (too cold!)
    too big (the gravity would squash you!)
    too small (the atmosphere would fly away!)

Think of the Earth, a tiny ball of rock
rushing round an ordinary star
far out on the spiral arm of an ordinary galaxy.

But here, now, on this tiny spinning ball

There's you.

Think how unlikely that is.

See just how special you are?

Rosemary Badcoe

THe AGeD SuN

Whether our star, the sun, grows old
by turning into liquid gold

And dripping down invisible space
to some celestial fireplace,

Expands, like science says it must,
and turns its planets into dust,

Or simply ups and disappears
like some ascending-ending spheres,

I do not think it matters much:
Great things destroy, depart, lose touch

When slow time reckons they are done –
and so it will be with the sun.

J Patrick Lewis

WHAT STARS ARE

Stars are not
  the shards of glass
    smashed by the gods in anger.
Neither are they
  the sparkling souls
    of intergalactic travellers.
They're not even
  the blinking eyes
    of invisible skywatchers.
No.
  Stars
      are
        stars.

The dying embers
  of ancient fires
    that will never know
      how they dazzle
        and delight us
          with the final flickers
            of their lives.

James Carter

HOW MANY MOONS THERE ARE!

The sail of a boat afloat on the dark,
The tailfin of a great white shark,
A funny punctuation mark –
How many moons there are!

An ice cream scoop, a pudding spoon,
A bowl of soup, a wrinkled prune,
A ballet shoe, a silk cocoon –
How many moons there are!

An elephant's trunk, a pelican's bill,
A slithery snake, a feathery quill,
A frozen lake, a fish's gill –
How many moons there are!

A postage stamp, a bony knee,
A shepherd's crook, a cup of tea,
Just take a look and you will see
How very, very, very, very many moons
    there are!

Graham Denton

HOMe

A marvel
of a marble, more
stable than a star, more
magical than moonshine, more
beautiful by far. Go search this big
blue marble, go see what Time
has grown – it's us, it's life, it's
living. It's Earth, it's here,
it's home.

James Carter

MYSTERIES OF THE UNIVERSE

We went by coach
to the planetarium
and saw the mysteries
of the universe.

We saw the birth of stars
black holes,
comets trailing cosmic dust,

and talked about
the existence of aliens.

But a greater mystery
awaited us all.

When we left school
sixty-two of us
boarded the coach.

When we arrived back at school
sixty-three of us got off.

Roger Stevens

MOON THEORY

Some scientists set out to prove
the moon is made of cheese;
the evidence they discover means
that everyone agrees

The surface of the moon
has bubbled into craters
caused, they think, by heating cheese
that's been through giant graters

Satisfied that they are right,
the scientists now boast
that some day soon, they're sure to find
a planet made of toast.

Celia Warren

TiMe IS eATiNG THe CLiFFs

RiDDLe

My first is in water, but isn't in air,
My second's in ocean and sea, but not there.
My third's in a river but not in a vale,
My fourth is in stream, not moor, hill
   or dale.
My fifth can be seen in a ditch – not a street –
And my whole can be found under everyone's
   feet.

Alison Chisholm

WHAT IS THE WORLD?

A scientist may say:
"70% water, 30% land."

A geologist may say:
"4.6 billion years old."

An astronomer may say:
"The merest speck on a cosmic coast
    awash in the tide of time."

A myth-maker may say:
"A glorious globe, suspended by four
    elephants atop a turtle."

A priest may say:
"A miracle."

An astronaut may say:
"Home."

An ecologist may say:
"Poorly."

James Carter

EARTH'S CLOCK

Imagine that the earth was shaped
twenty-four hours ago.
Then at 6am rains fell from the skies
to form the seas below.
At 8am in these soupy seas
the first signs of life appeared.
The dinosaurs called seventy minutes ago
but at twenty to twelve disappeared.
Man arrives just one minute ago
then at thirty seconds to midnight,
raised himself from his stooping stance
and started walking upright.
In the thirty seconds man's walked the earth
see what he's managed to do.

Earth's clock continues ticking:
the rest is up to you.

Pat Moon

VOLCANO

Silent dreamer
warning steamer
grumbling waker
island-maker!
Molten mountain
firework fountain
lava-spewer
earth-renewer

Sue Cowling

TiMe IS EATING THE CLiFFS

Time is eating the cliffs,
Slowly digesting them.

Come snow, come rain,
High tide and low,

Grain after grain,
Come breeze, come gale,

Come ice, come sun,
Time is eating the cliffs.

For a small while
Time will allow

Grasses to grow
In cracks of the cliffs,

Flowers to show
Their bright brave faces,

And will slyly reveal
The ancient hieroglyphs,

The curves and spirals,
The tough, ridged braille

42

Of ammonites, belemnites
Entombed aeons ago –

Fossil remains
To remind you of this:

That day by day,
Bite by tiny bite,

Time, who made the cliffs,
Is eating them away.

Gerard Benson

CHALK

As we walk across this hill of chalk
it's hard to imagine
that once these hills
were below the sea
that chalk is the sediment
left by a million tiny creatures
on the sea bed
it's hard to imagine
as we walk upon this thin skin
of earth and grass
beneath a blue sky
and a burning sun

Roger Stevens

OPPOSITES ATTRACT

Ice-cube Boy and Fire Girl
both fell in love at school.
Ice-cube Boy thought she was hot,
and she thought he was cool.
But when they tried to hug and kiss
her flame went 'fizzle!' 'pop!' and 'hiss!'
and Ice-cube Boy was turned to steam,
evaporating with a scream.
Their parents cried, "Our son! Our daughter!
Nothing more than smoke and water.
Now it's clear, it's just a fact –
opposites should *not* attract!"

Paul Hughes

CLOUDs Like us

You're n e v e r lonely as a cloud
for like the sheep, you're with the crowd.
And then there's always loads to do
like soak a fête or barbeque.

Clouds are water – boiled you know.
We're recycled H_2O.
Stream to sea to cloud to rain
ever moving through a chain.

How we love it when it's warm
for then we cook a mighty storm.
And when it's time to help the flowers
we'll brew up some April showers.

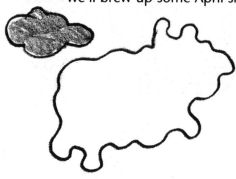

46

Going back to our CV –
we've a range of skills you see
snow to hail to mist to fog
and forming shapes for you to spot!

Sunny spell? Oh, we'll be back.
You'll need some rain – and that's a fact.
We're high as kites and cool as jazz.
That's clouds like us – our life's a gas!

James Carter

47

WHAT IS WATER?

A magician
transforming deserts
with a lick of its tongue.

A conjuror
coating ponds with ice
or brushing your cheek with mist.

A wild animal
plunging over cliffs,
breaking bridges and flooding valleys.

A healer
quenching thirst,
rekindling the seed's flame.

A slippery customer
slithering through your fingers,
always on the run.

John Foster

THIRTEEN THINGS TO DO WITH A RAINBOW

Keep it up for a skipping rope.
Throw it like a boomerang.
Put it on your head and wear it as a hairband.
Climb to the top and slide down the other
    side.
Sew it into shirts and form Rainbow United
    Football Club.
Turn it upside down to make yourself a boat.
Pour each of its colours into seven biro-refills
    so you'll have a fresh pen for every day of
    the week.
Cut lengths of it to wrap up birthday presents
    for your favourite people.
Paint concrete, grey days and elephants
    with it.
Wear it as a scarf in winter.
Weave it into a strong rope to take on a
    dragon hunt.
Wind it round a disused lighthouse to make a
    helter skelter.
Don't let it out of your sight.

David Horner

DARk, DARk, LiGHT

All light is starlight –
even the moon is only a mirror
reflecting the sun.

All light is starlight?

Deep in the oceans
an angler fish dangles
a glowing fishing rod.

A cookiecutter shark
camouflages
with a pale blue-green glow.

Squid squirt
shining clouds
of sticky mucus.

Down in the depths
too deep for sunlight
the sea is dark

except where lights
are glowing and confusing,
glimmering and scaring,
dancing, shimmering,
sparkling.

Rosemary Badcoe

SHADOW TALK

Psst!
It's me: your
shadow! I can
speak as well
you know.
I thought
it's
time to
say HELLO ... tell you things
you ought to know. Yes, we're
close   but far apart. For   unlike
you   I have no heart: or soul,   or
eye,   or lung, or bone. Like   Sister
Moon,   I'm cold as stone, and   born
of   night and lack of light. That   Mother
Sun?   She's way too bright! So after   dusk
the   time is mine, to drink the dark   like
thick   black wine. I wait till late   to
tear   away, to jump the roof   -tops,
off to play. Midnight
mischief. Spooky stuff.
Haunting   houses.
Nothing   rough.
Night's   my day
I think   you'll find.
Night's   so right
for shadow   -kind.
You can't   escape
– I'm here   to stay.
I'm behind   you
all the   way!

James Carter

HOW COME BEES CAN FLY?

FOSSILS

Older than
books,
than scrolls,

older
than the first
tales told

or the
first words
spoken

are the stories

in forests that
turned to
stone

in ice walls
that trapped the
mammoth

in the long
bones of
dinosaurs –

the fossil
stories that begin
Once upon a time

Lilian Moore

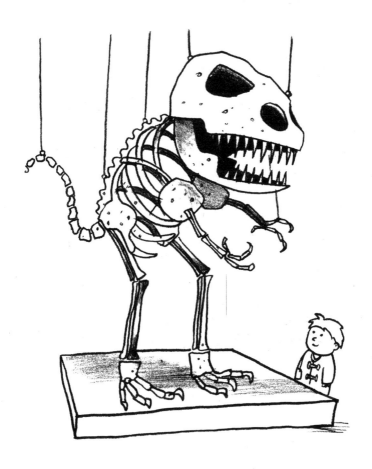

A FISH

A fish crawled out of the ocean
and flopped around in the sand
and he told his friend
that the latest trend
was amphibious life on land.

But his fishy friend was unconvinced
he said that he couldn't agree
he reckoned the shore
was a bit of a bore
and he'd stay as a fish in the sea.

Tom Stanier

THE MISSING LINK

I'm watching a programme about Darwin
And his theory of evolution –
How we all evolved from monkeys
But there's a missing link, somewhere,
    apparently.

I think I've found it – my brother.
He's called Simon which sounds like simian
And what does simian mean?
It means monkey-like.
And if you need further proof,
He does indeed like bananas.
He's always climbing trees.
And he looks just like the monkeys on the telly
The way he picks his nose,
Scratches his bum,
And does that funny face thing with curling lips.

"Simian!" I shout, ('cos that's what I call him
    now),
"You're on TV!"
He comes running in, sees what I'm watching.
He screeches and throws things at me
Just like the monkeys on the telly.

Amanda Lowe

THE GREAT DINOSAUR MYSTERY

Dinosaur, dinosaur,
where did you go?
Lost in a blizzard
and buried in snow?
Burned by volcanoes?
Killed by disease?
Starved by a terrible
shortage of bees?
Robbed by the mammals
who nibbled your eggs?
Choked by the gases
that swirled round your legs?
Or was it an asteroid
aimed at the earth
that ended your reign
and made way for our birth?

Clare Bevan

ZEBRA

Who let them loose
with face paints?
Who gave them pyjamas
to wear?
Who made them look
like newspapers?
Who striped them
here and there?

Who designed them
like mint humbugs?
Who painted them
white and black?
Who thought of
a different pattern
for each new
zebra's back?

Moira Andrew

CATERPILLAR

Once a chubby caterpillar
Sat upon a leaf,
Singing, "Eat, eat and be merry –
Life is very brief."

Soon he lost his appetite
And changed his merry tune.
He started spinning, hid himself
Inside a hard cocoon.

And he was still and quiet there –
Day after day went by.
At last it cracked and he emerged,
A gorgeous butterfly.

He spread his brown and crimson wings
And warmed them in the sun
And sang, "Now I must see the world –
My life has just begun."

Wendy Cope

HOW COME BEES CAN FLY?

A nervous bee panics
at aerodynamics,
so slight and so slender his wing,
while the bee's heavy torso
suggests, all the more so,
that flight's an impossible thing.

Yet the bee will survive
when he flies from the hive,
this worker without any money,
for practice defies
what theory implies
and the Queen Bee will still make her honey.

Celia Warren

BULB

Smooth fingers touch my papery skin,
place me in soil
in a shallow hole, cover me.

Loam and grains soothe,
and trickling water comforts.

I rest; seem dead, but only sleep.
I wait.

All at once, a tingle urges
slender threads to slip from me,
roots to feed me,
roots to anchor me.

And then my head surges
and a shoot, green as a frog,
forces up through earth,
reaches the light.

I shall burst with brilliance,
a blazing trumpet of daffodil
blaring at the sun.

When my yellow fades
to crisp parchment, I shall stay
in my secret cavern,
know worm and beetle,
feel my strength return
for next year's flowering.

Alison Chisholm

INVITATION FROM A MOLE

come on down

live among worms awhile
taste dirt
          on the tip of your tongue

smell
          the sweet damp feet of mushrooms
listen to roots
                    reaching
                              deeper

press your cheek against
the cold face of a stone

wear the earth like a glove
close your eyes
wrap yourself in darkness

          see

what you're missing

Alice Schertle

SNAIL TRAIL

Snail,
I love your silver trail,
the way it rambles all around
and glistens on the ground.

It seems to hold the magic of the moon.
For, see, it shimmers with a silken light
as if it stole its radiance in the night.
But how, the secret snail will never tell,
and, if you ask, retreats into its shell.

Yet, in the dark, who knows what subtle
    dance
the snail performs in strange, slow-motion
    trance,
brought on by radiant influence of the moon,
or prompted by its own internal tune,

to leave this mystic rune, this curious knot,
that gleams with meaning, though we know
    not what…?

Tony Mitton

Not a Tree

Not a tree – a trawler
Trapping sunshine in a green net.

Not a tree – a jailer
Locking light up tight in wood.

Not a mine – an escape route
Letting buried forests out of caves.

The black oil, the shiny coal
Are fragments of the sun.
They are the family of light
Waiting for the match, the flare
To give their warmth back to the air.

Jan Dean

WRapped in SkiN

Alphabod

Ankle bones are well connected
Brainwaves – aren't they grand?
Circulation's tireless.
DNA's a double strand.
Eyelids are a blinking marvel.
Fingerprints reveal us.
Goosebumps give a silent warning.
Hands can tend and heal us.
Indigestion? See a chemist!
Joints are versatile.
Knees have shock absorbers.
Lips look lovely in a smile.
Memory likes playing tricks.
Nose hair traps a fly.
Ossicles sound small and friendly.
Palms can prophesy.
Quadriceps are fearsome foursomes.
Ribs come neatly paired.
Speech is great – communicate!
Tonsils can be spared.
Unique.
Virtuoso –
Who can I be talking to?
Xtraordinary creature. Yes, I'm looking at
YOU (and you're ama-
Zing!)

Sue Cowling

WHEN GOD GAVE OUT NOSES

When God gave out noses
I thought He said "Roses"
so I asked for a big red one.

When He handed out legs
I thought He said "Eggs"
so I asked for two, hard-boiled.

When He gave out looks
I thought He said "Books"
so I said I didn't want any.

When He gave out brains
I thought He said "Trains"
and so I missed mine.

Anon

I Take Me For Granted

I take me for granted,
My cortex, my skin,
A membrane of mystery
That's holding me in.

My archway of eyebrows,
My tongue and my ears,
My speckles of freckles,
My colour, my tears.

My veins like a river,
My liver – a pearl,
My chromosomes name me,
A boy or a girl.

My heart – a silk engine,
Both fragile and strong,
My chorus of blood cells,
A cherry red song.

My lungs – a ribbed grotto
As confirmed by X-Ray,
Unparalleled fortune
Of my DNA.

I take me for granted,
What exactly's a gland?
Such things I don't know…
Like the back of my hand.

Stewart Henderson

BACTERIA

There are tens of thousands
on each one of us –
tinier than the tiniest fly,
so light we can't feel them.
Yet there they are –
like plump cows or sheep,
the colour of thin milk,
wandering across the broad fields of our skin
between the huge reeds of our hair,
nibbling.
And I like to think of them there
so calmly browsing, cleaning me up.
It makes me feel like a farmer, or more,
strangely, like the land itself, a world,
to have so many creatures
keeping alive on me,
so many creatures
that think of me as home.

Dave Calder

CHROMOSOME POEM

Each chromosome is home
To many genes
(The body's biological machines)
That tell you if your eyes
Are brown or blue,
Determine sizes
Of your hat, your shoe,
And tell you if your hair
Will wave or frizz.
The chromosomes sort out
The Hers from His
By making you
A Mr or a Ms.

J Patrick Lewis

WRappeD iN SkiN: A BODY RaP

Now check this out
this thing I'm in
this chunk of life
all wrapped in skin

Chorus (after every other verse)
Yeah, wrapped in skin
from head to toe
need all these things
to make me go

A skeletal frame
that creaks and groans
them joints, them ribs
them knees, them bones

You hear my heart?
You hear that thump?
it's for my blood –
it's like a pump

These muscles, man,
they help me move
for when I walk
or stand or groove

These two big lungs
go out an' in
to feed my blood
with oxygen

These kidneys too
I need them, see
to take my drink
and make my wee!

This great big brain
behind these eyes
keeps me thinkin'
keeps me wise!

Got all this stuff
and more besides
and you have too –
they're your insides!

James Carter

MY UNCOMMON Senses

I touch the taste
and I taste the sound.
Today my senses are
the wrong way round.

I can see the smell.
I can hear the view.
Today my senses
are all askew.

So I hear how you feel
and I smell what you say.
My senses are really
quite strange today.

David Bateman

I Asked the Little Boy That Cannot See

I asked the little boy that cannot see,
"And what is colour like?"
"Why green," said he,
"is like the rustle when the wind blows
    through
the forest; running water, that is blue;
and red is like a trumpet sound; and pink
is like the smell of roses; and I think
that purple must be like a thunderstorm;
and yellow is like something soft and warm;
and white is a pleasant stillness when you lie
    and dream."

Anon

AN ODE TO MY BRAIN

You're a schemer.
You're a dreamer.
You're the bit
that makes me me.

You're all spongey.
You're all gungey.
And you help me
feel and see.

You sit inside
my head up here.
You drive me around.
You help me hear.

You're creative.
You're inventive.
You're the bit
that makes me tick.

You're a tiny
little library.
You're the thing
that makes me think.

For a grown-up
or a baby
you're amazing...ly
BRAINY!

James Carter

VALENTINE FROM A SCIENTIST

It's not in your heart but in your head
That stops you from acting inane
It's in the head that you feel fear
Or love or hate or pain.
The heart has nought to do with emotions,
It merely pumps blood through your veins.
So it might not sound romantic but
I love you with all my brain.

Celina Macdonald

A Sci-Fi DReaM

AMazing inventions

When I was 10
I really believed
that in the future
there'd be
such **AMAZING INVENTIONS** as
    FLYING CARS
    UNDERWATER CARS
    MACHINESthatcouldmakeanyflavour*crisp*youaskedfor
day trips to the MOON
video phones
and robot dogs (& cats)
in e v e r y home
and
MOST IMPORTANTLY
bubble gum
that can make you INVISIBLE

So you can imagine
just how d i s a p p o i n t e d I was
when I got to 20
and none of them
had come true

So you can also imagine
how e x t r e m e l y m i f f e d I was
when I got to 40

and still none of them
had come true

Until they do
I'd like to say
do you know what
                    I reckon
is *THE MOST* **AMAZING INVENTION**
us humans have come up with so far?

Have a think.

Our brains
                    come up with them
Our mouths
                    get rid of them
This poem
                    is made of them.

James Carter

I WENT TO THE FUTURE

I went to the future,
stayed a week in a space hotel.
Met a boy who told me
no one one ever got sick now
and all wars were gone.
He showed me a photo
of a family of dodos,
talked about his alien friend,
then suggested I join him
on a day-trip to the moon.

I went to the future,
stood there under a purple sun.
The buildings were silver
and no one walked the streets
in the icy wind.
I saw dead trees,
dogs that were half lion,
an artificial ozone layer.
It was the wrong future,
it wasn't mine.

I went to the future,
met the President of the Moon.
He asked if I wanted to live there,
said the air was clean.
He threw me a happiness ball.

I held it and smiled.
He struck up a tune
on the one-stringed zumbo
and I knew then I wanted to
follow him to the moon.

Matthew Sweeney

MY ROCKET DREAMED

My rocket dreamed of circling the Earth,
orbiting the moon,
zigzagging planets,
looping the loop with satellites
dodging meteorites
racing comets
and disappearing into time warps and
    black holes.

Instead, it circled the garden shed,
orbited the swing,
zigzagged the apple tree,
looped the loop with the clothes line,
dodged two butterflies,
raced one wasp and a bluebottle,
then disappeared over the hedge
into the time warp and black hole
that is Mr Hislop's back garden.

Paul Cookson

THE OWL AND THE ASTRONAUT

The owl and the astronaut sailed through
  space
in their intergalactic ship
they kept hunger at bay
with three pills a day
and drank through a protein drip.

The owl dreamed of mince
and slices of quince
and remarked how life had gone flat.
"It may be all right
to go faster than light
but I preferred the boat and the cat."

Gareth Owen

JUMPING ON THE MOON

When you jump on Earth
you land with a thud
in the mud

When you jump on the moon
you soar like a balloon
you glide like a feather
on a summer afternoon
you float like a ballet dancer
in a graceful arc
you land like a dandelion clock
in the park

Roger Stevens

PUZZLiNG!

Don't

a

in

space

jigsaw

out

do

those

float

place

bits

all

over

will

the

James Carter

UNKNOWN WORLDS

Zooming on and on and on,
The Earth, the moon, the sun long gone.
Scorching on through time and space
In wild galactic star-wars race.

Our world a zillion miles behind,
Who knows what fantasies we'll find?
Travelling where no human's been
Except in night-time, sci-fi dream.

Constellations flashing past
With blue-blurred speed of laser blast.
Adventures wait light-years ahead
Beyond our wildest dreams in bed.

Will aliens bang on rocket door
With Zodiacal chill-blood roar?
Will Darth Vader or E.T.
Come cruising in on cosmic sea?

Aquarius dawns, the past long gone,
The future waits as we zoom on.
Goodbye, goodbye, the world we knew,
Oh unknown worlds we come to you.

Clive Webster

HeY, Science!

STOP.

An answer please.

We need one of your **theories**.
You've told us how it all began.
With nothing. Then a great ***big bang!***

And how the sun and moon were made
and what you think the world must weigh.
Of atoms, yes, and **gravity**
and how the oceans came to be.

Then land, then life, then wheel, then car
then trips to Mars and **blah blah blah**.
But what we want to know and how –
is why the world's so really... **WOW?**

The honey bee? The polar bear?
The platypus? Or don't you care?
The thrill, the spill, the thing you feel
at sunset on a snowy hill?

A summer sky, an autumn wood –
oh why on earth's the world this **good?**
This little rock on which we dwell:
the chance of life? Well, who can tell?

So take your time to ponder it
and look around the world a bit.
Or peep into your microscope.
Your answer will be good. **We hope**.

James Carter

ACKNOWLEDGEMENTS

All poems have been included with kind permission of the authors.

'Chalk' by Roger Stevens first appeared in *The Monster That Ate the Universe* by Roger Stevens, published by Macmillan Children's Books, 2004.

'I Take Me for Granted' by Stewart Henderson was commissioned by BBC Radio 4 for the series *Wide Awake at Bedtime*, first broadcast January 2008.

'Jumping on the Moon' by Roger Stevens first appeared in *Space Poems* chosen by Gaby Morgan, published by Macmillan Children's Books, 2006.

'Moon Theory' by Celia Warren first appeared in *Funny Poems* selected by Jan Dean, published by Scholastic, 2003.

'What Stars Are' by James Carter first appeared in *Greetings, Earthlings* published by Macmillan Children's Books, 2009.

'Mysteries of the Universe' by Roger Stevens first appeared in *I Did Not Eat the Goldfish* by Roger Stevens, published by Macmillan Children's Books, 2002.

'My Uncommon Senses' by David Bateman first appeared in *Sensational! Poems Inspired by the Five Senses* chosen by Roger McGough, published by Macmillan Children's Books, 2004.

'Riddle' by Alison Chisholm first appeared in *Elements in Poetry: Poems About Earth* compiled by Andrew Fusek Peters, published by Evans Brothers Ltd, 2004

'Thirteen Things to Do with a Rainbow' by David Horner first appeared in *Mmmmm* by David Horner, published by Apple Pie Publications, 1997.

'Time Is Eating the Cliffs' by Gerard Benson first appeared in *To Catch an Elephant* by Gerard Benson, published by Smith/Doorstop, 2002.

'What Is Water?' by John Foster first appeared in *Standing on the Sidelines* by John Foster, published by Oxford University Press, 1995.

'Amazing Inventions' by James Carter first appeared in *Time-Travelling Underpants*, published by Macmillan Children's Books, 2007.